Ulo Florack

Ulo Florack

The Woodruff Key

Jewellery and Objects

Arnoldsche Art Publishers

Essay by Beatriz Chadour-Sampson
Photography by Andreas Brücklmair
Typographic design by Mathias Berschet

Forthcoming Exhibitions

Deutsches Goldschmiedehaus Hanau
20 January to 7 April 2013

Kreismuseum Zons, Dormagen
21 April to 30 June 2013

Maximilianmuseum, Augsburg
14 July to 13 October 2013

Contents

Between Fantasy and Reality

The work of Ulo Florack

Beatriz Chadour-Sampson

Mysterious and fantastical figures and creatures, sometimes half man and half animal or magical inscriptions feature in Ulo Florack's jewellery and objects. The imagery is exaggerated with grimaced faces, burlesque, farcical or monster-like figures and mythical beasts. The representation of our world is distorted and reflects the artist's state of mind and his perception. Ulo Florack creates his personal images of reality, filtered through his soul. Each of the pieces makes reference to his personal life, and to everyday experiences, or even current events. Florack confesses he has had to come to terms with the fact that he cannot simply make an object or piece of jewellery. His creations are reflections of his inner soul, thus he could never work to commission. Florack uses symbols and metaphors, often intermingled with an element of wit or certain critique.

Florack takes inspiration from his immediate environment. People, objects, animals or everyday events capture his imagination. He puts himself into the role of the observer, and emerging from this viewpoint lets his emotions initiate the artistic process. The moment of creation begins, as soon as Florack feels the urge to sketch something

Zwischen Fantasie und Realität

Die Arbeiten von Ulo Florack

Beatriz Chadour-Sampson

Die Darstellung rätselhaft-fantastischer Figuren und mythischer Gestalten, halb Mensch, halb Tier, aber auch magische Inschriften sind kennzeichnend für Ulo Floracks Schmuckarbeiten und Kunstobjekte. Die Bildhaftigkeit wird akzentuiert und übertrieben durch grimassierende Gesichter, burleske, possenhafte oder monsterhafte Figuren und mythische Tiergestalten. Wie in einem Vexierspiegel wird die Verzerrung unseres momentanen Weltempfindens in der Wahrnehmung und dem ganz eigenen Blick des Künstlers gekonnt zurückgeworfen. Ulo Florack erschafft sich seine eigenen Bilder der Realität, gefiltert aus seinem Innersten. Jedes Objekt nimmt Bezug auf Floracks persönliche Lebensumstände, auf alltägliche, oft brandaktuelle Begebenheiten. Wie er freimütig bekennt, musste er sich erst daran gewöhnen, dass er nicht einfach so ein Kunstobjekt oder ein Schmuckstück herstellen kann. Die Werke entstehen aus ihm, aus seiner innersten Seele heraus – dies ist mit einer der Gründe, warum er niemals auf Anfrage arbeiten könnte. Aus seinen Objekten, die vordergründig ausschließlich mit Metaphern und Symbolen spielen, sind Humor, Witz und die Beobachtungsgabe eines kritischen Geistes nie wegzudenken.

on paper, or feels compelled to model the wax in his hands. It is only after having finished a piece, that its true significance or deeper meaning becomes apparent to him.

Modelling materials is what comes most naturally to Florack, rather than instinctively drawing lines on paper. He feels the process of modelling is more spontaneous, and the outcome is quicker than making a drawing. It is the search in his innermost being that helps him find the solution to an idea. Florack admits that before he reaches his goal, he goes through a rollercoaster of ups and downs. Ideas are condemned then defended, destroyed then saved before reaching what he defines as a storm and stress period. All his work has undergone this arduous journey.

Visually his pieces may at first appear primitive or archaic, but this is a deception. On close examination the complexity of the goldsmithing techniques and his attention to detail is easily detected. The work processes he applies are meticulous and arduous, requiring great skill. Florack's work is full of dualities and contradictions. Its expressionist style stands in stark contrast with his precise execution and almost perfectionist goldsmithing techniques. The imagery is deceptively primitive, the content, though, is mythical and mystical. He never reveals the secret messages of his themes and symbols, nor the personal resonance of his compositions. Rather he leaves it to the viewer's imagination to interpret the stories and to disentangle the meanings within the symbolism. Magic lies in the unknown.

Although they are cast, all of Florack's jewellery and objects are one-off pieces. This method normally associated with mass

Florack lässt sich von seiner unmittelbaren Umwelt inspirieren. Menschen, Objekte oder Tiere wie auch alltägliche Ereignisse regen seine Fantasie an. Sein Blick ist derjenige eines distanzierten Beobachters, und von dieser Sicht aus werden seine Emotionen ausgelöst, die den künstlerischen Prozess anspornen. Dieser beginnt mit dem Drang, etwas auf Papier zu bringen, oder Florack sieht sich gezwungen, seinen Händen mit dem Modellierwachs freien Lauf zu lassen. Aber erst, wenn ein Objekt fertiggestellt ist, manifestiert sich für den Künstler seine wahre Bedeutung und sein tieferer Sinn.

Das Arbeiten in Wachs oder ähnlich formbaren Materialien entspricht Floracks Naturell mehr noch als die intuitive Zeichnung, da der spontane Modelliervorgang den Künstler mit einem schnelleren Ergebnis belohnt. Es ist die Reise zu seinem Innersten, die ihn immer eine Lösung finden lässt. Florack bekennt, der Weg zu seinem Ziel ist wie eine Achterbahn voller Höhen und Tiefen. Ideen werden verdammt, dann wieder verteidigt, zerstört und wieder gerettet – und dann erst folgt die eigentliche „Sturm und Drang"-Periode des Schaffens. Dieser beschwerliche und hindernisreiche Weg zieht sich durch sein ganzes Werk.

Der ursprüngliche Eindruck des Primitiven oder Archaischen in seinem Werk täuscht. Bei näherer Betrachtung werden die Komplexität seiner Goldschmiedetechniken und die konzentrierte Aufmerksamkeit auf Details sichtbar. Die angewendeten Arbeitsprozesse sind mühsam und minutiös genau, sie erfordern höchste Sorgfalt und großes Können. Die Arbeiten Floracks sind in ihrer Aussage zwiespältig und widersprüchlich. Der expressionistische Stil steht in starkem

production is applied here for very different reasons. Casting allows him to transform his ideas directly into wax models, his hands acting intuitively. Florack is fascinated by the malleability of various metals and alloys. It could be said that he thinks 'in metal' and the range which he uses – gold, platinum, silver, copper, iron and chrome-cobalt-alloys – is his 'playground'. Like an alchemist he has developed his own recipes for various alloys, for example, alloys made of platinum and gold, or copper and iron. He often adds 24 carat gold plating on cast silver. Occasionally remnants from antique objects are inserted to form a link with the past and to shed new light on an old theme.

Colour plays a major role in his compositions, and vivid colours in enamel enhance his work. The application of enamel gives him great pleasure and enjoyment, a feel of artistic freedom; Florack, the painter, comes to the fore. The choice of colour is arbitrary and made on the spur of the moment, depending on his emotions. Colours reflect the state of his inner soul. He describes the enamelling process, as follows: 'I literally fly over my palette of colours and take what I feel drawn to.' He is a brilliant colourist, and rarely uses gemstones.

Florack is primarily a maker of jewelled objects. However, jewellery is central to his work and within this finger rings dominate. In his view rings only need to meet one requirement that is to encircle the finger, and therefore the design variations are limitless. Rings are for him almost like human beings with a soul. They are given a personality and he hopes that during their lifetime they may find a wearer. The wearability of his rings is of no concern to him, they simply fall into

Kontrast zur präzisen Ausführung und zu den fast schon perfektionistisch anmutenden Goldschmiedetechniken. Die Bildersprache ist nur auf den ersten Blick täuschend archaisch, inhaltlich ist sie jedoch mythisch und mystisch. Florack gewährt in seinen Werken weder Einblick in deren geheime Aussagekraft noch in eine irgendwie geartete persönlich gefärbte Resonanz. Es bleibt dem Betrachter überlassen, die abgebildeten Inhalte zu interpretieren und die Deutung der eingesetzten Symbolik zu entflechten. Diese spezielle Magie liegt gänzlich im Ungewissen.

Die Schmuckstücke und Objekte sind fast alle gegossen und doch sind sie alle einzigartig. Diese Methode, die eigentlich aus der Massenproduktion stammt, wird hier einer komplett anderen Vorstellung untergeordnet. Das Modellieren in Wachs ist ein intuitiver Prozess, nur die Hände „sprechen". Offenkundig ist Floracks Faszination für die Verformbarkeit der Metalle und Legierungen. Er denkt sozusagen „in Metall", sei es nun in Gold, Platin, Silber, Kupfer, Eisen oder Chrom-Kobalt-Verbindungen, und gleichzeitig sind diese Materialien ein Spielplatz für seine Kreativität. Wie ein Alchemist alter Schule stellt er seine Rezepturen für Legierungen aus Platin und Gold oder Kupfer und Eisen selbst her. Oft werden Silbergüsse noch 24-karätig vergoldet. Gelegentlich werden Elemente von antiken Objekten verarbeitet, die eine Verbindung zur Vergangenheit schaffen und gleichzeitig neues Licht auf eine zeitlose Thematik werfen.

Farbe spielt in seinen Kunstobjekten eine bedeutende Rolle, und die lebhaft leuchtenden Farben des Emails steigern die Schmuckarbeiten. Das Auftragen des Emails gibt ihm eine besondere Freude, aber zugleich auch ein

the realm of sculpture or treasures placed in a cabinet.

Ulo Florack is an artist of many talents and almost impossible to classify. The question of whether he is a painter or a jeweller remains unanswered, both media nurture each other. His jewellery is sculptural and the application of colour painterly. Florack's style is unmistakable and his jewellery full of ideological and intellectual metaphors, hovering between reality and fantasy.

Müstair
wood, branding
2008

Stück künstlerische Freiheit: Der Maler Florack rückt in den Vordergrund. Die Wahl der Farben ist willkürlich, ganz der Eingebung des Augenblicks oder der gefühlsmäßigen Befindlichkeit geschuldet. Die Farben spiegeln die Seele des Künstlers wider. Den Arbeitsgang des Emaillierens beschreibt er so: „Ich fliege buchstäblich über der Farbpalette und nehme, was immer mich anzieht." Er benutzt Farben auf brillante Art und Weise, nur selten werden Edelsteine verwendet.

In erster Linie stellt Florack Schmuckobjekte her, der Schmuck rückt ins Zentrum seines Schaffens, und in diesem Zusammenhang sind vor allem Ringe dominant. Da Ringe nach seiner Sicht der Dinge nur das Umschließen des Fingers als Voraussetzung erfüllen müssen, sind die Designvarianten grenzenlos. Ringe sind für ihn fast so etwas wie Lebewesen mit einer Seele. Sie besitzen eine eigene Persönlichkeit und Florack hofft, dass sie während ihres Lebens einen „passenden" Träger finden. Ob die Ringe letztlich tragbar sind oder nicht, spielt für ihn keine Rolle. Sie werden als Skulptur sowie Kunstwerk aufgefasst und ihr ausschließlicher Verbleib in einer Vitrine wäre ebenfalls denkbar.

Ulo Florack ist ein vielfältig talentierter Künstler. Es ist so gut wie unmöglich, ihn zu klassifizieren. Die Frage, ob er eher Maler oder Schmuckkünstler ist, kann nicht entschieden beantwortet werden; beide Bereiche befruchten sich gegenseitig. Seine Schmuckobjekte verinnerlichen die Idee der Skulptur, Art und Aufbringung der Farben verraten den Maler. Sein Stil ist unverwechselbar und seine Objekte überraschen mit einer ideologischen und intelligenten Metaphorik, die bewusst in der Grauzone zwischen Fantasie und Realität schwebt.

et jamais au lit avant
deux heures du matin
object
1

please give me back
my stone
ring
2

armed forces
brooch
3

for dolores
napkin ring
4

bamboo
pin box
5

l' homme il se
macère dans le gout
ring

there is always
somebody faster
ring
7

invest on the wall
brooch
8

birthday roll
pendant
9

money for nothing,
chicks for free

rings

dochti
ring
11

sluggard
ring
12

neque id quare fieri
non possit …
ring
13

Kremlecka
pile of rings
14

Lisnabrin
ring
15

by pure chance
object
16

prior tempore potior iure
ring
17

pikeldy
ring
18

fleur de Florác
ring
19

Gründungsnagel
three-piece can
22

cinq centimes l'an 7
pendant, amulet
23

bathing scene with servant and screen
3 pendants, 1 object
24

having a whale of time
brooch
25

flacón
object
26

scene of companions
pendants
27

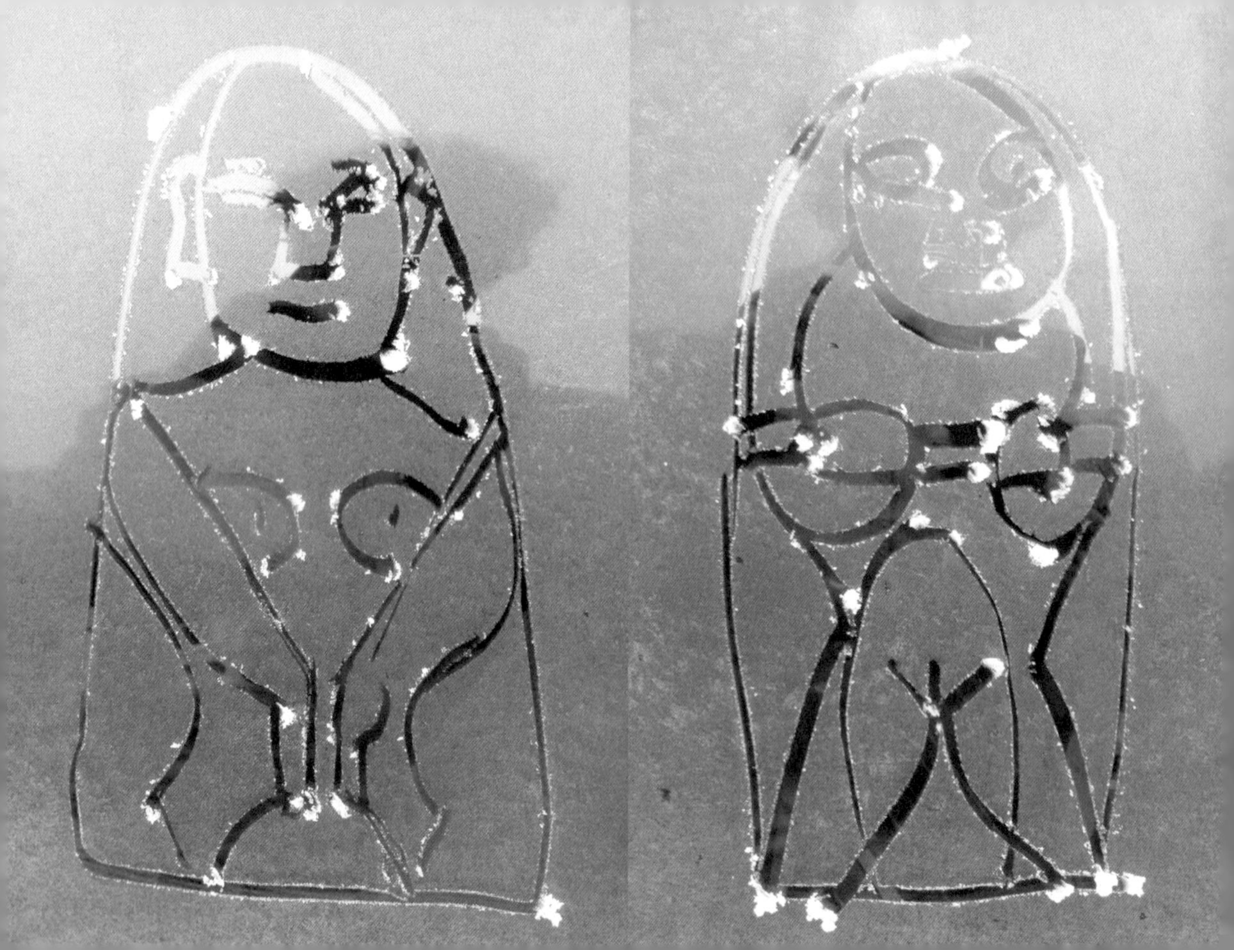

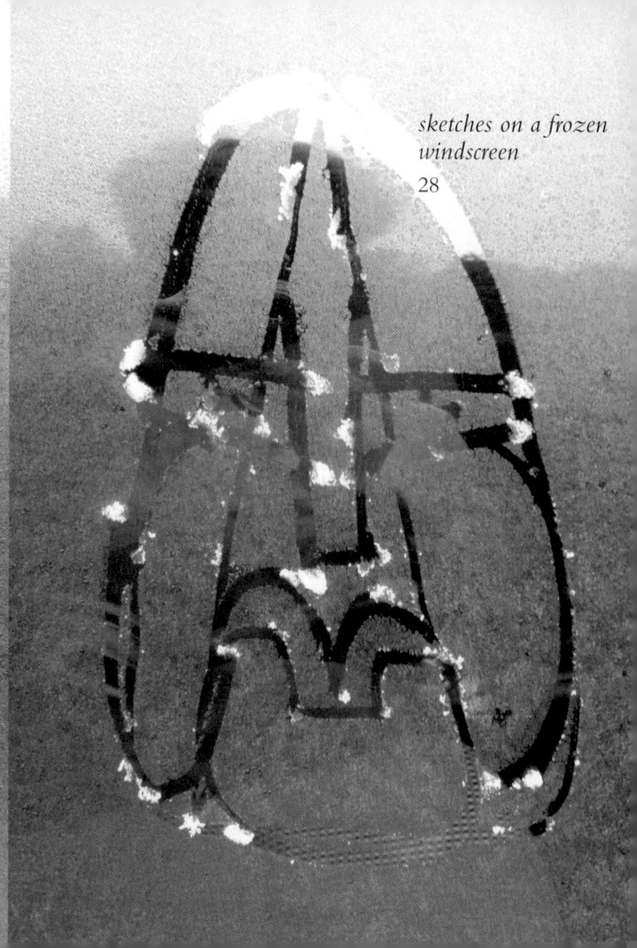

sketches on a frozen windscreen
28

je suis tombé en désuétude
ring
29

isseki nichô
ring
30

mobile antenna
ring
31

mundus vult decipi
ring
32

rings to come (wax)
33

casting details, working files
34

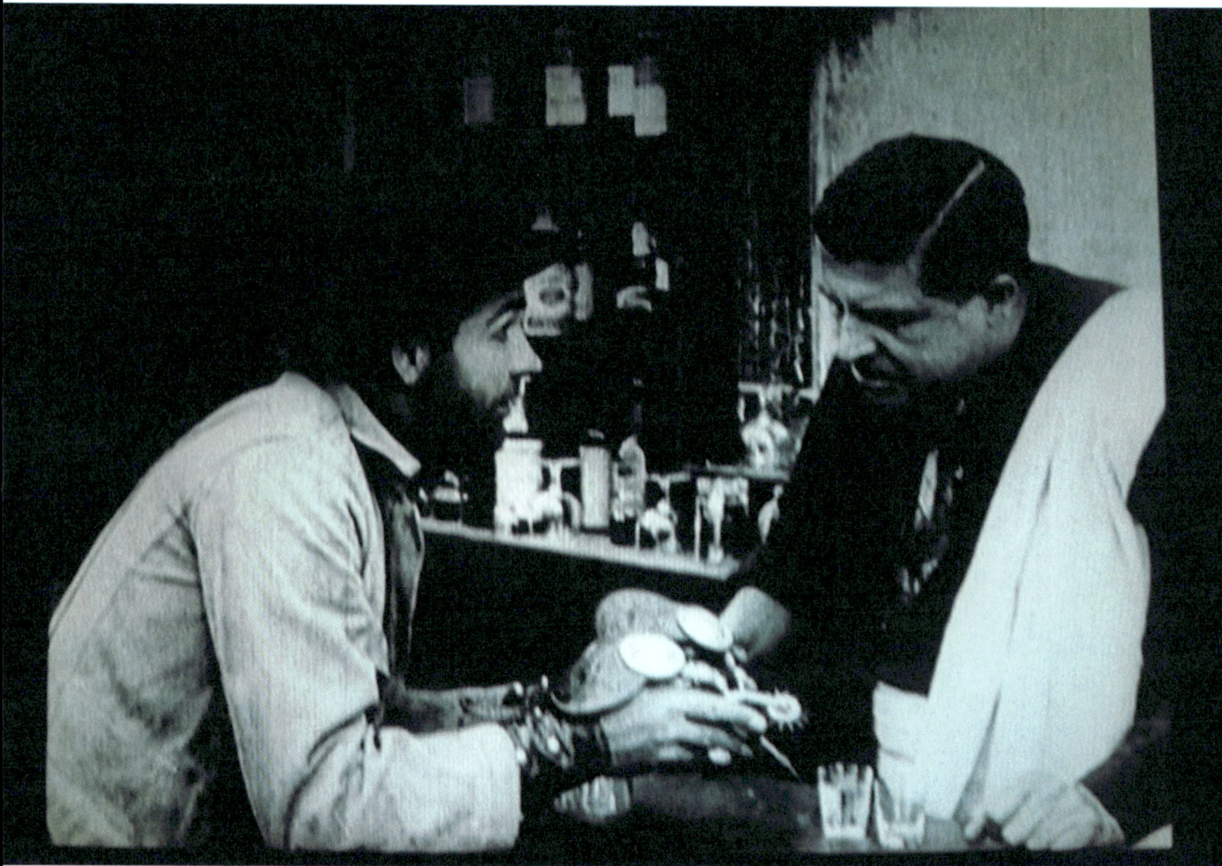

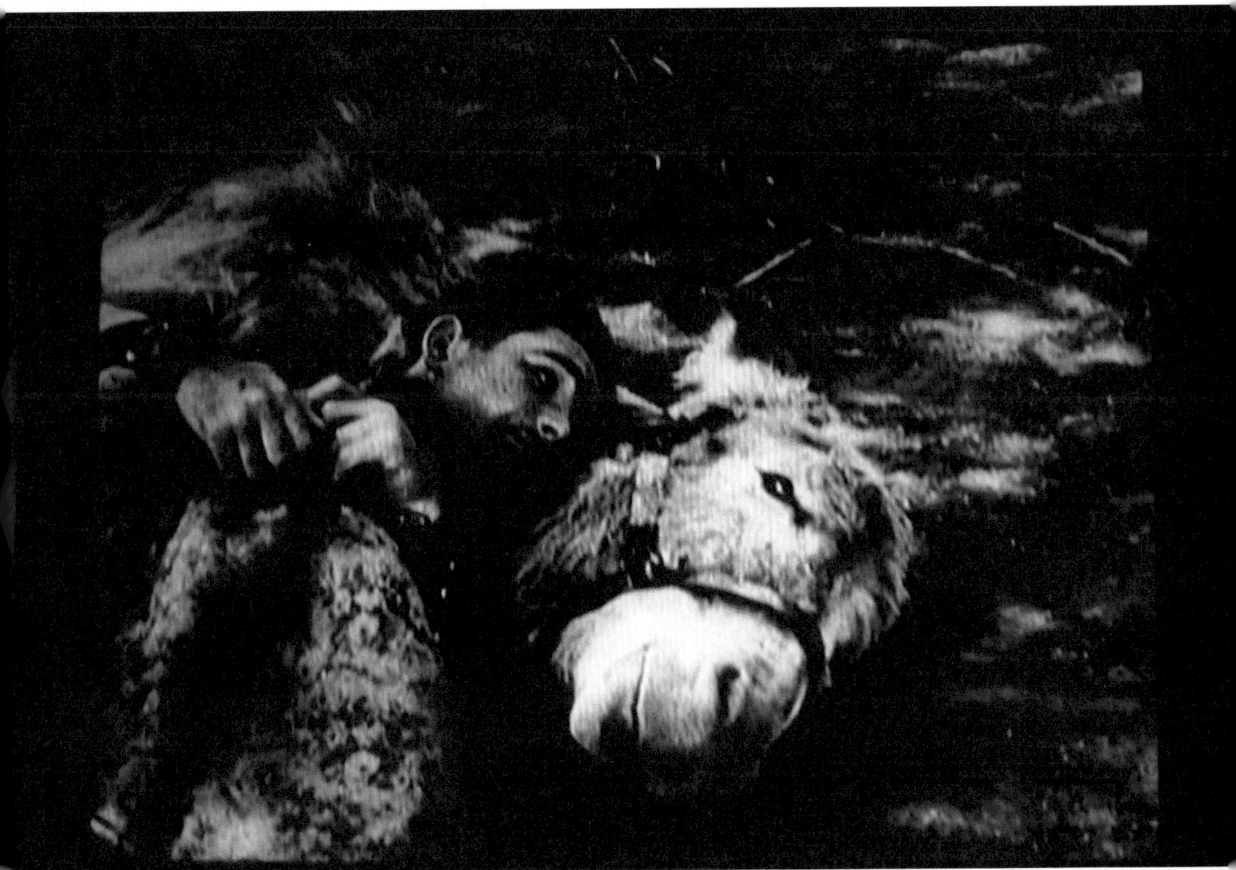

charivari
necklace
36

courier
brooch
37

best knight
brooch
38

to do the right thing
brooch
39

buccaneer
brooch
40

sightseeing tour
brooch
41

fire for granted
brooch
42

autodafé
brooch
43

Kursk
brooch
44

magic mechanic
ring
45

Honda Cub 50 ohc
Knockadoon Head
46

ship arriving too late
to save a drowning witch
brooch
21

balance of a dowser
object
20

date under water

bird's palace
brooch
48

walk the dog
brooch
49

Blaukopf
brooch
50

Amazone kocht
brooch
51

best boy
brooch
52

pour la vitesse
brooch
53

cauldron
brooch
54

Saddam's dog
brooch
55

la rouge de honte
brooch
56

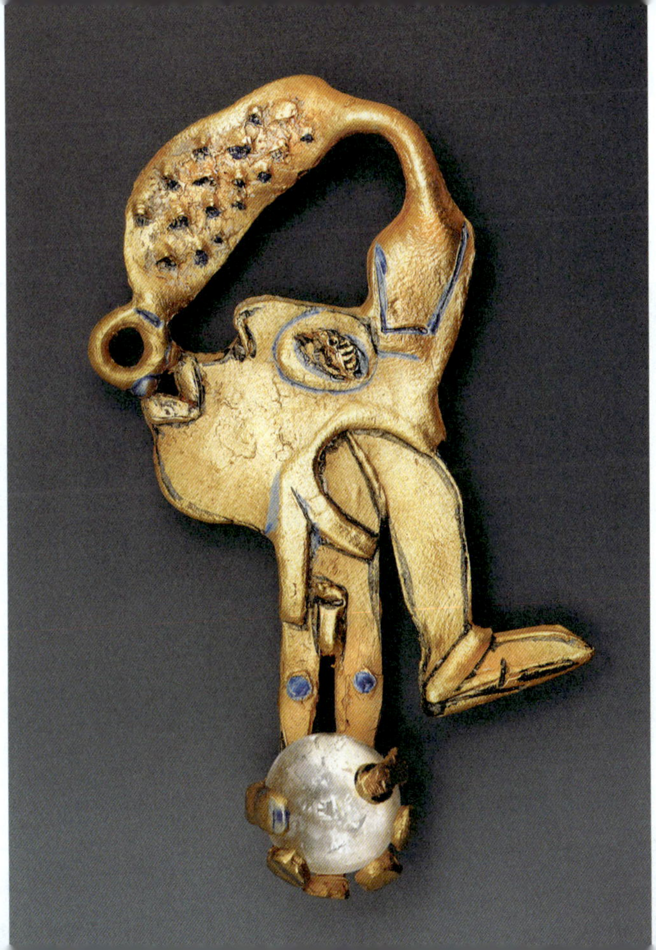

one shot
brooch
57

man's jewels

3 Döschen
59

nuts

Mr and Mrs Crab
objects
61

home of Crab jr.
62

workshop
63

ceterum censeo
object
64

boule set
65

shinto priest
ring
66

life could be worse
ring
67

second choice
ring
68

réunion
ring
69

Kinga
ring
70

every tube has its secret
ring
71

it is part of our Scottishness
ring
72

et mihi dulce magis resoluto
vivere collo
ring
73

Mauskovitz
ring
74

Korybanten
ring
75

three on a sledge
brooch
76

all those people invited

RT – two
bracelet
78

Crab's friend
brooch
79

no command
pendant
80

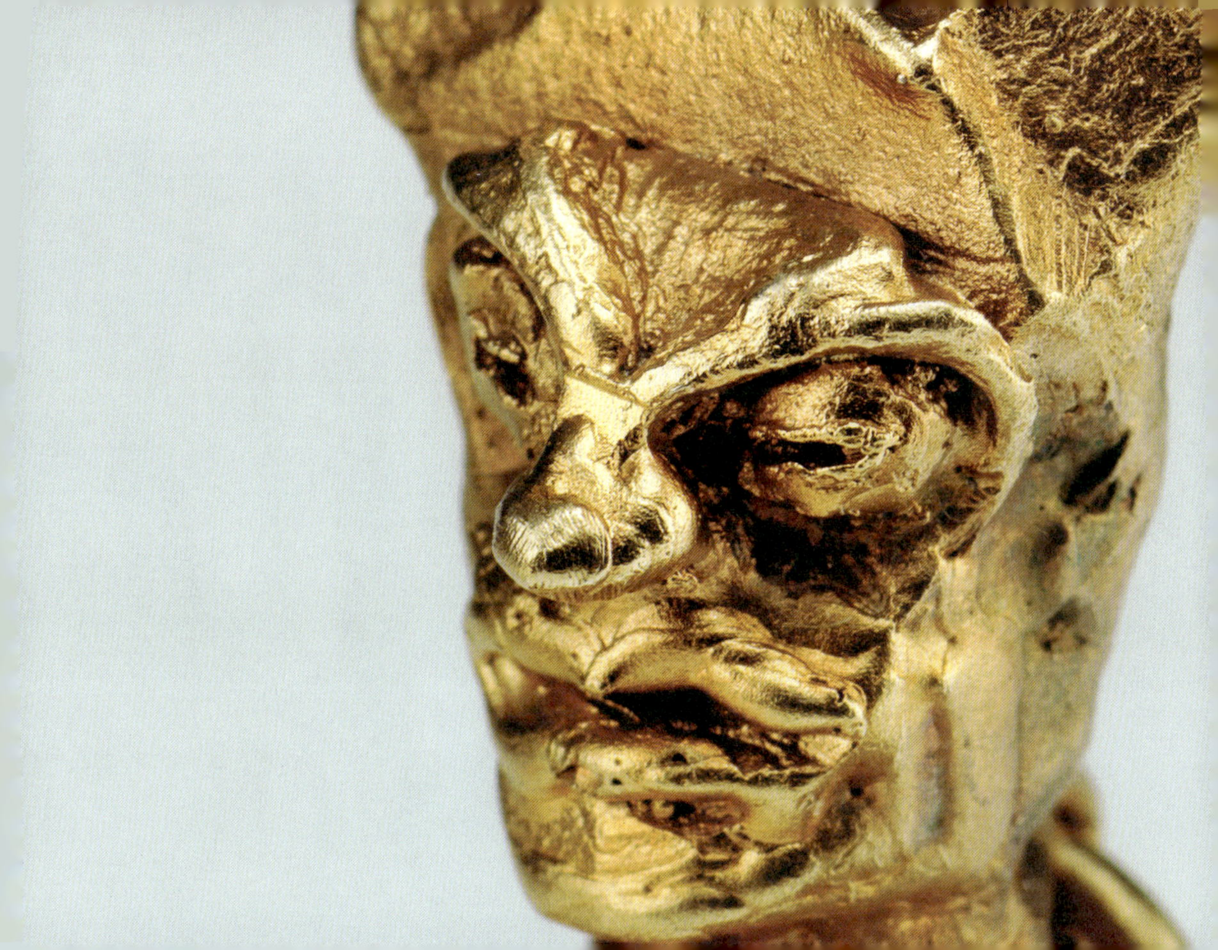

earpins
81

Schüttung 2010
82

Ulo Florack | CV Jewellery

1958 Born in Augsburg (D)
1983 Munich Academy of Fine Arts (Professor Hermann Jünger and Professor Jörg Immendorff)
1989 Diploma (Hermann Jünger)
Since 1989 freelance goldsmith and painter, lives and works in Augsburg and County Cork, Ireland

Exhibitions

1987 Österreichisches Landesmuseum, Linz (A)
1988 Galerie Marzee, Nijmegen (NL)
Galerie Spektrum, Munich (D)
1989 Galerie für Modernen Schmuck, Frankfurt (D)
1990 Galerie für Modernen Schmuck, Frankfurt (D)
Galerie Treykorn, Berlin (D)
Danner-Preis '90, Bayerisches Nationalmuseum, Munich (D)
1991 5. Triennale, Kestnergesellschaft, Hannover (D)
Kunstgewerbemuseum, Frankfurt (D)
Nationalmuseum, Leipzig (D)
1993 „Münchner Goldschmiede", Münchner Stadtmuseum, Munich (D)
1993 „Schmuck und Gerät", Galerie Hurlimann, Zurich (CH)
Galerie Knauth und Hagen, Bonn (D)
Danner-Preis '93, Bamberg, Residenz (D)
„Pour le mérite", V+V Galerie, Vienna (A)
1994 „Contes colorés du royaume d'or", Galerie Knauth und Hagen, Bonn (D)
1996 Galerie Helga Malten, Dortmund (D)
Art Hill Center, Seoul (KOR)
1997 Galerie Louise Smit, Amsterdam (NL)
Galerie Hermann Hermsen, Wiesbaden (D)
1998 Galerie Aurum, Frankfurt (D)
Galerie Helga Malten, Dortmund (D)
Sofa Art Fair, New York (USA)
1999 Danner-Preis '99, Regensburg (D)
Galerie Ventil, Munich (D)
Galerie Profil, Regensburg (D)
Galerie Birgitta Knauth, Bonn (D)
2000 Kunsthaus Kaufbeuren (D)
„hautnah", Künstlerhaus, Vienna (A)
8. Triennale, MAK Frankfurt (D)
„Schmuck aus München", Deutsches Goldschmiedehaus Hanau (D)

2002 „Jewelry in painting", Mobilia Gallery, Cambridge (USA)
„teapot redefined", Mobilia Gallery, Cambridge (USA)
Sofa Art Fair, New York (USA)
„annuale", Barockart Galerie, Schloss Markt Wald (D)
„5 gramm gold", Galerie Aurum, Frankfurt (D)

2003 „Sonderschau Schmuck", Internationale Handwerksmesse München (D)
„brachium ecclesiasticum", V+V Galerie, Vienna (A)
„Valuable Links", jewels from the OSZE countries in Maastricht (NL)

2004 „Valuable Links", jewels from the OSZE countries in Sofia (BGN)

2005 Danner-Preis '05, Bayerisches Nationalmuseum, Munich (D)

2006 Internationale Handwerksmesse München (D)
Galerie Handwerk, Munich (D)

2007 „Amulett + Talisman", Galerie Ventil, Munich (D)
„Vitrine", V+V Galerie, Vienna (A)

2008 „Isseki Nichô", Galerie Aurum, Shopstop 4, MAK Frankfurt (D)
„Künstlerisches Spielzeug – spielerische Kunst", Galerie Handwerk, Munich (D)

2009 „Künstlerisches Spielzeug – spielerische Kunst", Galerie Handwerk, Munich (D)

2010 Villa Bengel, Idar-Oberstein (D)
Galerie für Kunst und Design, Pforzheim (D)
„Lingam", Stockholm (SE), Utrecht (NL), Mons (BE)
„Künstlerisches Spielzeug – spielerische Kunst", Galerie Handwerk, Munich (D)

2011 „Masala 1", Ecke Galerie, Augsburg (D)
Danner-Preis '11, Munich (D)
„Künstlerisches Spielzeug – spielerische Kunst", Galerie Handwerk, Munich (D)

2012 „Die Renaissance des Emaillierens", Galerie Handwerk, Munich (D)
Symposium 2012, Turnov (CZ)

2013 „The Woodruff Key", Deutsches Goldschmiedehaus Hanau (D), Kreismuseum Zons, Dormagen (D), Maximilianmuseum, Augsburg (D)

Collections

Collection Abeler (D)
Collection Alice and Louis Koch (CH)
Die Neue Sammlung – The International Design Museum, Munich (permanent loan from the Danner Foundation, Munich) (D)
Collection Villa Bengel, Idar-Oberstein (D)
Collection Museum Turnov (CZ)

Awards

1989 Kunstförderpreis der Stadt Augsburg (D)
1990 Prix jeune peinture étranger, Paris – Künstlergruppe „Freibank“ (F)
1991 Kunstförderpreis der Stadt Augsburg – Künstlergruppe „Freibank“ (D)
2004 Arno-Buchegger-Preis, Augsburg (D)
2007 Ecke-Kunstpreis, Augsburg (D)
2011 Danner-Ehrenpreis, Munich (D)
Arno-Buchegger-Preis, Augsburg (D)

Index

s. s. a. means „special silver alloy"

1 *et jamais au lit avant deux heures du matin*
object, silver alloy, 2006
size: 79 × 47 × 28 mm

2 *please give me back my stone*
ring, 925 silver, 2012
piece of bohemian pine root, chrome-diopsit
size: 94 × 32 × 44 mm
Collection Museum Turnov (CZ)

3 *armed forces*
brooch, s. s. a., acrylic-paint, steel pin, 2010
size: 82 × 69 × 36 mm

4 *for dolores*
napkin ring, s. s. a., enamel, 1997
size: 40 × 48 × 41 mm
Collection Karcher (D)

5 *bamboo*
pin box, carved and coloured, 2010
size: 148 × 39 × 40 mm

6 *l'homme il se macère dans le gout*
ring, s. s. a., enamel, gilded, 2008
size: 72 × 25 × 40 mm

7 *there is always somebody faster*
ring, s. s. a., enamel, 2012
size: 84 × 27 × 28 mm

8 *invest on the wall*
brooch, japanese investment, coloured, steel pin, 2012
size: 75 × 54 × 15 mm

9 *birthday roll*
pendant, dough, resin, fine silver, 2005
size: 64 × 53 × 30 mm
chain length: 680 mm

10 *money for nothing, chicks for free*
a) ring, s. s. a., enamel, gilded, synthetic ruby, carved and engraved on the inside, 2012
b) ring, s. s. a., enamel, gilded, printed in wax and cast, 2012
size a): 31 × 23 × 39 mm
size b): 29 × 23 × 39 mm

11 *dochti*
ring, s. s. a., enamel, ancient glass with screwed setting, 2012
size: 41 × 29 × 28 mm

12 *sluggard*
ring, s. s. a., enamel, 2012
size: 48 × 23 × 31 mm

13 *neque id quare fieri non possit …*
ring, s. s. a., enamel, gilded, garnets, 2012
size: 65 × 36 × 67 mm

14 *Kremlecka*
3 rings as a pile
on top: fine silver, enamel, 2012
size: 27 × 22 × 12 mm
middle: s. s. a., enamel, 2012
size: 22 × 21 × 10 mm
bottom: s. s. a., enamel, 1997
size: 27 × 26 × 13 mm

15 *Lisnabrin*
ring, s. s. a., enamel, chestnut, bark artefact, 2010
size: 58 × 26 × 28 mm

16 *by pure chance*
object, silver alloys, 2012
size: 39 × 104 × 22 mm

17 *prior tempore potior iure*
ring, s. s. a., enamel, iron, 2012
size: 60 × 26 × 23 mm

18 *pikeldy*
ring, s. s. a., enamel, 2012
size: 50 × 23 × 19 mm

19 *fleur de Florác*
ring, s. s. a., enamel, 2010
size: 39 × 26 × 26 mm

20 *balance of a dowser*
pendant, silver alloy, gilded, 2008
size: 78 × 60 × 37 mm

21 *ship arriving too late to save a drowning witch*
brooch, s. s. a., steel pin, 2007
size: 78 × 78 × 28 mm

22 *Gründungsnagel*
three-piece can, fine silver, enamel paint, fine gold, part of ancient nail, reassambled it will be a closed can, 2005
size: 40 × 22 × 22 mm

23 *cinq centimes l'an* 7
pendant, amulet, fine silver, fine gold, coin, ancient glass, 2006
size: 54 × 54 × 15 mm

24 *bathing scene with servant and screen*
3 pendants, 1 object, s. s. a., enamel, gilded, 2 garnets, 2008
size bathtube: 28 × 41 × 23 mm
size animal: 40 × 27 × 31 mm
size servant: 35 × 15 × 18 mm
size screen: 24 × 15 × 15 mm

25 *having a whale of time*
brooch, s. s. a., enamel, gilded, 1998
size: 50 × 58 × 12 mm

26 *flacón*
object, s. s. a., enamel, gilded, 2007
removable top, cork stopper underneath
size cap: 22 × 15 × 15 mm
size flacón: 39 × 33 × 12 mm

27 *scene of companions (7 out of 12)*
pendants, synthetic rubies, carved, engraved, 2009 – 2010
size: about 46 × 20 × 13 mm

28 *sketches on a frozen windscreen*
2009

29 *je suis tombé en désuétude*
ring, s. s. a., enamel, 2008
size: 42 × 30 × 16 mm

30 *isseki nichô*
ring, s. s. a., enamel, gilded, rider, s. s. a., enamel, 2008
size: 62 × 51 × 13 mm
Collection Abeler (D)

31 *mobile antenna*
ring, s. s. a., enamel, 2002 – 2009
size: 49 × 22 × 18 mm

32 *mundus vult decipi*
ring, s. s. a., enamel, 2004
size: 31 × 26 × 27 mm

33 *rings to come (wax)*
example of waxmodells ready for casting, 2012

34 *casting details, working files*

35 *as life rolls on*
The photographs have been printed with the express permission of those who have reserved all rights to them. Nevertheless despite all efforts made, the authors of some photographs could not be found. In such cases we ask that the owners contact us.

36 *charivari*
necklace with 49 objects, 2005
variety of alloys, e.g. gold, platinum, silver, copper
length: 540 mm

37 *courier*
brooch, s. s. a., enamel, gilded, steel pin, 1994
size: 54 x 39 x 9 mm

38 *best knight*
brooch, s. s. a., fine gold, enamel, settingplate 925 silver, steel pin, 1997
size: 59 x 62 x 7 mm

39 *to do the right thing*
brooch, s. s. a., enamel, gilded, steel pin, two-piece, figure rotating, 2009
size: 45 x 45 x 25 mm

40 *buccaneer*
brooch, s. s. a., enamel, gilded, steel pin, 2010
size: 50 x 43 x 12 mm

41 *sightseeing tour*
brooch, s. s. a., enamel, gilded, 1997
size: 32 x 48 x 12 mm

42 *fire for granted*
brooch, s. s. a., enamel, gilded, steel pin, 2002
size: 57 x 63 x 7 mm

43 *autodafé*
brooch, s. s. a., enamel, 2 rubies, gilded, setting frame 925 silver gilded, steel pin, 1998
size: 51 x 67 x 27 mm

44 *Kursk*
brooch, s. s. a., enamel, partly gilded, object coming out of the porthole gold-platinum alloy, 2004
size: 41 x 45 x 11 mm

45 *magic mechanic*
ring, s. s. a., partly gilded, 2010
size: 52 x 14 x 11 mm

46 *Honda Cub 50 ohc, Knockadoon Head, Ireland*
picture of a bike slowly eaten and extinguished by the Irish Sea, 2012

47 *date under water*
picture of the artist, 2012

48 *bird's palace*
brooch, s. s. a., enamel, gilded, steel pin, 2010
size: 49 x 54 x 42 mm

49 *walk the dog*
brooch, s. s. a., enamel, gilded, steel pin, 2010
size: 60 x 65 x 17 mm

50 *Blaukopf*
brooch, s. s. a., enamel, gilded, steel pin, 2010
size: 60 x 78 x 45 mm
Collection Gallery for Art and Design, Pforzheim (D)

51 *Amazone kocht*
brooch, s. s. a., enamel, gilded, steel pin, 2010
size: 49 x 50 x 9 mm

52 *best boy*
brooch, s. s. a., enamel, partly gilded, fine gold rivets, steel pin, 2009
size: 46 x 46 x 3 mm

53 *pour la vitesse*
brooch, s. s. a., enamel, gilded, 10 rubies, steel pin, 1998
size: 52 x 52 x 12 mm

54 *cauldron*
brooch, s. s. a., enamel, partly gilded, steel pin, 2010
size: 53 x 48 x 10 mm

55 *Saddam's dog*
brooch, s. s. a., enamel, gilded, 2 garnets, chrome-cobalt alloy, gold alloy, steel pin, 1996
size dog: 36 x 49 x 26 mm
size cage: 45 x 54 x 45 mm

56 *la rouge de honte*
brooch, s. s. a., enamel, gilded, steel pin, 2008
size: 56 x 38 x 23 mm

57 *one shot*
brooch, s. s. a., rock crystal, enamel, gilded, 2007
size: 77 x 45 x 20 mm

58 *man's jewels*
gloves, belt with chrom-cobalt buckle, flail, silver alloy, rock crystal cathead, 1999 – 2009

59 *3 Döschen*
s.s.a., enamel, 1996 – 2011
size (left to right):
47 x 20 x 21 mm
45 x 22 x 23 mm
43 x 18 x 18 mm

60 *nuts*
walnuts, acrylic paint, 2006 – 2008
nutsize

61 *Mr and Mrs Crab*
objects
Mr Crab: stone, fishbone, crab-claw, seaweed, silver pendant, wood, 2010
size: 132 x 66 x 60 mm
Mrs Crab: crabshell, 925 silver, crabclaw, wood, 2010
size: 63 x 105 x 58 mm
flacon: s. s. a., enamel, gilded
size: 33 x 15 x 15 mm

62 *home of Crab jr.*
wooden scene, wood of orange tree, birch-bark, lobster skin, seaweed, antique ceramic, heather, seeds of tropic plant, 2011
size: 275 x 365 x 130 mm

63 *workshop*
wooden scene, wood of orange tree, rock crystal, ancient bronze, fishbone, bamboo, 2011
size: 195 x 380 x 130 mm

64 *ceterum censeo*
object, silver alloy, gilded, 2005
size: 47 x 40 x 47 mm

65 *boule set*
9 steel balls, etched, 1996
size big: Ø 49 mm
size small: Ø 26 mm

66 *shinto priest*
ring, s. s. a., enamel, iron, 2008
size: 43 x 25 x 6 mm

67 *life could be worse*
ring, silver-platinum-copper alloy, 2012
size: 43 x 23 x 26 mm

68 *second choice*
ring, s. s. a., partly gilded, 2009
size: 25 x 21 x 22 mm

69 *réunion*★
ring, gold-platinum alloy, enamel, 2004
size: 25 x 25 x 18 mm

70 *Kinga*
ring, s. s. a., superstructure: galvanic finesilver gilded, 2008 – 2012
size: 78 x 47 x 44 mm

71 *every tube has its secret* ★
ring, s. s. a., enamel, gilded, 1998
size: 75 x 38 x 40 mm

72 *it is part of our Scottishness*
ring, s. s. a., fine gold, 3 alexandrites, padparatscha ruby, 1998
size: 33 x 27 x 24 mm

73 *et mihi dulce magis resoluto vivere collo*
ring, s. s. a., fine gold, enamel, 2010
size: 44 x 24 x 24 mm

74 *Mauskovitz* ★
ring, galvanic fine silver, enamel, 2001
size: 60 x 20 x 12 mm

75 *Korybanten*
ring, s. s. a., fine gold, enamel, 2003
size: 26 x 24 x 24 mm

76 *three on a sledge*
brooch, silver alloy, steel pin, 2007
size: 32 x 42 x 12 mm

77 *all those people invited*
acrylic paint on canvas, 1989
size: 310 x 170 cm (detail)

78 *RT – two*
bracelet, s. s. a., partly gilded, 2010
size: 49 x 63 x 38 mm

79 *Crab's friend*
brooch, s. s. a., enamel, partly gilded, steel pin, 2010
size: 92 x 48 x 24 mm

80 *no command*
pendant, silver alloy, gilded, 2007
size: 120 x 55 x 32 mm

81 *earpins*
variety of alloys, e.g. gold, platinum, silver, copper, 1996 – 2005

82 *Schüttung 2010*

★ Die Neue Sammlung – The International Design Museum, Munich (permanent loan from the Danner Foundation, Munich) (D)

Imprint

Editor: Ulo Florack, Augsburg, www.klimt02.net

Author: Beatriz Chadour-Sampson, London

Translation: Christina Hirson, Augsburg

Text editing: Christiane Kühn, Augsburg

ARNOLDSCHE *project coordinator:* Marion Boschka

Image and text editing: Ulo Florack, Augsburg

Typographic design: Mathias Berschet, Augsburg

Photography: Andreas Brücklmair, Augsburg;
Index 71: Jürgen Meister, Munich; Index 48, 49, 50: Eva Jünger, Munich;
Index 28, 33, 34, 46: Ulo Florack, Augsburg

Digital Imaging: Bruno Buè, Andreas Brücklmair

Printed by: Leibfarth & Schwarz, Dettingen/Erms

Paper: PlanoPak, 50 g/m^2, holzfrei, alterungsbeständig

Bound by: BELTZ Bad Langensalza GmbH, Bad Langensalza

Bibliographic information published by the Deutsche Nationalbibliothek
The Deutsche Nationalbibliothek lists this publication in the Deutsche Nationalbibliografie; detailed bibliographic data are available in the Internet at www.d-nb.de.

ISBN 978-3-89790-385-2

Made in Germany, 2013

For general questions, please contact ARNOLDSCHE Art Publishers directly at art@arnoldsche.com, or visit our website at www.arnoldsche.com for further information.

Special thanks to:

My private parc fermé (tapfer, tapfer), a system is a system, thank you so much Mathias, to royal photographer Andy, digital fighter Bruno, Beatriz Chadour-Sampson, company Dochtermann, interrogative, helpful Haul, Hans, Hella, Ute and Peter Renz, Doris Sacher, Oliver Kautz, Miroslav Cogan, Christianne Weber-Stöber, Angelika Riemann, Christoph Emmendörffer, Kristina Balzer, Christiane Kühn, Christina Hirson, Björn and Franzi, Anette and Wolfgang and many thanks also to Marion Boschka and Dirk Allgaier of Arnoldsche Art Publishers.

figure on the right:
into the crack of dawn
brooch, s. s. a., enamel, gilded, 2012
size: 36 × 24 × 24 mm

Produced with the generous support of:

Arno-Buchegger-Stiftung, Augsburg

Danner Stiftung

Danner-Stiftung, München

NEUER SCHMUCK

Fördergesellschaft Neuer Schmuck e.V.

Gesellschaft für Goldschmiedekunst e.V.
Deutsches Goldschmiedehaus Hanau

Künstlervereinigung Augsburg
„Die Ecke“

rhein kreis neuss

Kreismuseum Zons, Dormagen

kunstsammlungen
museen augsburg

chef has chilled out to sweeten his style